Count It Up Checkbook Register

A Simple Format Checkbook Record

George L. Babec

Count It Up Checkbook Register

Simple Format Checkbook Record

Copyright © 2014 by George L. Babec

ISBN: 1500756997

ISBN-13: 978-1500756994

First Edition: August 2014

CONTENTS

Page

Example Section   1

Check Registry Section   7

Savings Deposit Section   83

NOTICE

The example registers are for reference only and should not be considered to be any form of financial advice or guidance. The examples are simply depicting one possible method of entering personal financial transactions into the simple layout register tables.

Example Section

This section contains examples of how to make entries into the checking and savings registers. The large alternating gray and white lines make it very easy to enter debits and credits and to keep track of the current balance. Deposits are depicted by a plus sign preceding the entry.

Financial data can easily be written and read due to the large, simple format, registry fields.

Checking		Balance Forward:	
Date	Check #	Payee / Description	327.89
3/24		Local Market	145.77
			182.12
3/24		Local Bakery	18.45
		Honey Buns	163.67
3/25		Local Gas Station	45.32
		Van Gas	118.35
3/26		Paycheck Deposit	+795.34
			913.69
3/27	976	Local Golf Pro Shop	356.99
		New Set of Golf Clubs	556.70
3/28		Local Restaurant	56.78
		Breakfast	499.92
3/28	977	Post Office	5.79
			494.13
3/28		Local Golf Course	79.85
			414.28
3/29		Local Warehouse Club	49.95
		Membership	364.33
3/30		Count It Up Diet Journal	9.17
			355.16
3/30		Count It Up Workout	8.88
		Journal	346.28
3/31		Local Cave Tour	34.97
			311.31
		Ending Balance:	311.31

Savings		Balance Forward:	
Date	Description		$235.45
2/3	Deposit		+100.00
	From Checking		335.45
2/24	Deposit		+100.00
	Check #3456		435.45
3/4	Withdraw		125.00
			310.45
3/20	Deposit		+100.00
			410.45
3/29	Deposit		+234.78
	From Checking		645.23
4/5	Deposit		+456.00
			1101.23
4/7	Withdraw to Checking		277.78
			823.45
4/9	Deposit		+45.00
			868.45
4/28	Deposit		+78.56
			947.01
5/2	Deposit		+234.34
			1181.35
5/17	Withdraw to Checking		275.00
			906.35
5/19	Deposit		+100.33
			1006.68
		Ending Balance:	$1006.68

CHECK REGISTRY SECTION

This section contains the Checkbook Register pages. Refer to the Example Section for an explanation of how to use the pages.

Count It Up Checkbook Register

	Checking		Balance Forward:	
Date	Check #	Payee / Description		
		Ending Balance:		

Checkbook Register

Checking			Balance Forward:	
Date	Check #	Payee / Description		
		Ending Balance:		

Count It Up Checkbook Register

	Checking		Balance Forward:	
Date	Check #	Payee / Description		
			Ending Balance:	

Checkbook Register

Checking			Balance Forward:	
Date	Check #	Payee / Description		
			Ending Balance:	

Count It Up Checkbook Register

Checking			Balance Forward:	
Date	Check #	Payee / Description		
			Ending Balance:	

Checkbook Register

	Checking		Balance Forward:	
Date	Check #	Payee / Description		
			Ending Balance:	

Count It Up Checkbook Register

Checking		Balance Forward:	
Date	Check #	Payee / Description	
		Ending Balance:	

Checkbook Register

Checking		Balance Forward:	
Date	Check #	Payee / Description	
		Ending Balance:	

Count It Up Checkbook Register

	Checking		Balance Forward:	
Date	Check #	Payee / Description		
			Ending Balance:	

Checkbook Register

Checking			Balance Forward:	
Date	Check #	Payee / Description		
			Ending Balance:	

Count It Up Checkbook Register

Checking			Balance Forward:	
Date	Check #	Payee / Description		
			Ending Balance:	

Checkbook Register

	Checking		Balance Forward:	
Date	Check #	Payee / Description		
			Ending Balance:	

Count It Up Checkbook Register

Checking		Balance Forward:	
Date	Check #	Payee / Description	
		Ending Balance:	

Checkbook Register

Checking			Balance Forward:	
Date	Check #	Payee / Description		
		Ending Balance:		

Count It Up Checkbook Register

Checking			Balance Forward:	
Date	Check #	Payee / Description		
		Ending Balance:		

Checkbook Register

Checking			Balance Forward:	
Date	Check #	Payee / Description		
		Ending Balance:		

Count It Up Checkbook Register

Checking			Balance Forward:	
Date	Check #	Payee / Description		
			Ending Balance:	

Checkbook Register

Checking		Balance Forward:	
Date	Check #	Payee / Description	
		Ending Balance:	

Count It Up Checkbook Register

Checking			Balance Forward:	
Date	Check #	Payee / Description		
			Ending Balance:	

Checkbook Register

Checking			Balance Forward:	
Date	Check #	Payee / Description		
		Ending Balance:		

Count It Up Checkbook Register

Checking			Balance Forward:	
Date	Check #	Payee / Description		
		Ending Balance:		

Checkbook Register

Checking			Balance Forward:	
Date	Check #	Payee / Description		
			Ending Balance:	

Count It Up Checkbook Register

	Checking		Balance Forward:	
Date	Check #	Payee / Description		
			Ending Balance:	

Checkbook Register

Checking		Balance Forward:	
Date	Check #	Payee / Description	
		Ending Balance:	

Count It Up Checkbook Register

Checking			Balance Forward:	
Date	Check #	Payee / Description		
			Ending Balance:	

Checkbook Register

Checking			Balance Forward:	
Date	Check #	Payee / Description		
			Ending Balance:	

Count It Up Checkbook Register

Checking			Balance Forward:	
Date	Check #	Payee / Description		
		Ending Balance:		

Checkbook Register

Checking		Balance Forward:	
Date	Check #	Payee / Description	
		Ending Balance:	

Count It Up Checkbook Register

Checking			Balance Forward:	
Date	Check #	Payee / Description		
		Ending Balance:		

Checkbook Register

		Checking	Balance Forward:
Date	Check #	Payee / Description	
		Ending Balance:	

Count It Up Checkbook Register

	Checking		Balance Forward:	
Date	Check #	Payee / Description		
			Ending Balance:	

Checkbook Register

Checking			Balance Forward:	
Date	Check #	Payee / Description		
			Ending Balance:	

Count It Up Checkbook Register

Checking			Balance Forward:	
Date	Check #	Payee / Description		
			Ending Balance:	

Checkbook Register

Checking			Balance Forward:	
Date	Check #	Payee / Description		
			Ending Balance:	

Count It Up Checkbook Register

Checking			Balance Forward:	
Date	Check #	Payee / Description		
		Ending Balance:		

Checkbook Register

Checking			Balance Forward:	
Date	Check #	Payee / Description		
			Ending Balance:	

Count It Up Checkbook Register

	Checking		Balance Forward:	
Date	Check #	Payee / Description		
			Ending Balance:	

Checkbook Register

	Checking		Balance Forward:	
Date	Check #	Payee / Description		
			Ending Balance:	

Count It Up Checkbook Register

	Checking			Balance Forward:	
Date	Check #	Payee / Description			
			Ending Balance:		

Checkbook Register

Checking			Balance Forward:	
Date	Check #	Payee / Description		
			Ending Balance:	

Count It Up Checkbook Register

	Checking		Balance Forward:	
Date	**Check #**	**Payee / Description**		
			Ending Balance:	

Checkbook Register

Checking		Balance Forward:	
Date	**Check #**	**Payee / Description**	
		Ending Balance:	

Count It Up Checkbook Register

Checking			Balance Forward:	
Date	Check #	Payee / Description		
		Ending Balance:		

Checkbook Register

Checking			Balance Forward:	
Date	Check #	Payee / Description		
			Ending Balance:	

Count It Up Checkbook Register

Checking			Balance Forward:	
Date	Check #	Payee / Description		
			Ending Balance:	

Checkbook Register

Checking			Balance Forward:	
Date	Check #	Payee / Description		
			Ending Balance:	

Count It Up Checkbook Register

Checking			Balance Forward:	
Date	Check #	Payee / Description		
			Ending Balance:	

Checkbook Register

Checking		Balance Forward:	
Date	Check #	Payee / Description	
		Ending Balance:	

Count It Up Checkbook Register

Checking			Balance Forward:	
Date	Check #	Payee / Description		
		Ending Balance:		

Checkbook Register

Checking			Balance Forward:	
Date	Check #	Payee / Description		
		Ending Balance:		

Count It Up Checkbook Register

Checking			Balance Forward:	
Date	Check #	Payee / Description		
			Ending Balance:	

Checkbook Register

Checking			Balance Forward:	
Date	Check #	Payee / Description		
		Ending Balance:		

Count It Up Checkbook Register

Checking			Balance Forward:	
Date	Check #	Payee / Description		
			Ending Balance:	

Checkbook Register

	Checking			Balance Forward:	
Date	Check #	Payee / Description			
			Ending Balance:		

Count It Up Checkbook Register

Checking		Balance Forward:	
Date	Check #	Payee / Description	
		Ending Balance:	

Checkbook Register

Checking		Balance Forward:	
Date	Check #	Payee / Description	
		Ending Balance:	

Count It Up Checkbook Register

	Checking		Balance Forward:	
Date	Check #	Payee / Description		
			Ending Balance:	

Checkbook Register

Date	Check #	Payee / Description	Checking — Balance Forward:
		Ending Balance:	

Count It Up Checkbook Register

	Checking		Balance Forward:	
Date	Check #	Payee / Description		
			Ending Balance:	

Checkbook Register

Checking			Balance Forward:	
Date	Check #	Payee / Description		
		Ending Balance:		

Count It Up Checkbook Register

Checking		Balance Forward:	
Date	Check #	Payee / Description	
		Ending Balance:	

Checkbook Register

Checking			Balance Forward:	
Date	Check #	Payee / Description		
		Ending Balance:		

Count It Up Checkbook Register

Checking			Balance Forward:	
Date	Check #	Payee / Description		
			Ending Balance:	

Checkbook Register

Checking			Balance Forward:	
Date	Check #	Payee / Description		
		Ending Balance:		

Count It Up Checkbook Register

Checking		Balance Forward:	
Date	Check #	Payee / Description	
		Ending Balance:	

Checkbook Register

Checking			Balance Forward:	
Date	Check #	Payee / Description		
		Ending Balance:		

Count It Up Checkbook Register

	Checking			Balance Forward:	
Date	Check #	Payee / Description			
			Ending Balance:		

Checkbook Register

Checking			Balance Forward:	
Date	Check #	Payee / Description		
		Ending Balance:		

Count It Up Checkbook Register

Checking			Balance Forward:	
Date	Check #	Payee / Description		
		Ending Balance:		

Checkbook Register

		Checking		Balance Forward:	
Date	Check #	Payee / Description			
				Ending Balance:	

Count It Up Checkbook Register

Checking			Balance Forward:	
Date	Check #	Payee / Description		
		Ending Balance:		

Checkbook Register

	Checking			Balance Forward:	
Date	Check #	Payee / Description			
				Ending Balance:	

Count It Up Checkbook Register

Checking			Balance Forward:	
Date	Check #	Payee / Description		
			Ending Balance:	

Checkbook Register

Checking			Balance Forward:	
Date	Check #	Payee / Description		
			Ending Balance:	

Count It Up Checkbook Register

Checking			Balance Forward:	
Date	Check #	Payee / Description		
		Ending Balance:		

Checkbook Register

Checking			Balance Forward:	
Date	Check #	Payee / Description		
			Ending Balance:	

Count It Up Checkbook Register

Checking			Balance Forward:	
Date	Check #	Payee / Description		
			Ending Balance:	

Checkbook Register

Checking			Balance Forward:	
Date	Check #	Payee / Description		
			Ending Balance:	

Count It Up Checkbook Register

Checking		Balance Forward:	
Date	Check #	Payee / Description	
		Ending Balance:	

SAVINGS DEPOSIT SECTION

This section contains the Savings Register pages. Refer to the Example Section for an explanation of how to use the pages.

Count It Up Checkbook Register

Savings		Balance Forward:	
Date	Description		
		Ending Balance:	

Savings Deposits

Savings		Balance Forward:	
Date	Description		
		Ending Balance:	

Count It Up Checkbook Register

Savings			Balance Forward:	
Date	Description			
			Ending Balance:	

Savings Deposits

Savings		Balance Forward:	
Date	Description		
		Ending Balance:	

Count It Up Checkbook Register

Savings		Balance Forward:	
Date	Description		
		Ending Balance:	

Savings Deposits

Savings		Balance Forward:	
Date	Description		
		Ending Balance:	

Count It Up Checkbook Register

Savings		Balance Forward:	
Date	Description		
		Ending Balance:	

Savings Deposits

| Savings | | Balance Forward: | |
Date	Description		
		Ending Balance:	

Count It Up Checkbook Register

Savings		Balance Forward:	
Date	**Description**		
		Ending Balance:	

Savings Deposits

Savings			Balance Forward:	
Date	Description			
			Ending Balance:	

Count It Up Checkbook Register

| Savings | | | Balance Forward: | |
Date	Description			
			Ending Balance:	

Savings Deposits

Savings		Balance Forward:	
Date	**Description**		
		Ending Balance:	

Count It Up Checkbook Register

Savings		Balance Forward:	
Date	Description		
		Ending Balance:	

Savings Deposits

Savings		Balance Forward:	
Date	**Description**		
		Ending Balance:	

Count It Up Checkbook Register

Savings		Balance Forward:	
Date	Description		
		Ending Balance:	

Savings Deposits

Savings		Balance Forward:	
Date	Description		
		Ending Balance:	

Savings Deposits

Savings		Balance Forward:	
Date	Description		
		Ending Balance:	

Notes:

Related works:

Count It Up Workout Journal
ISBN-13: 978-1500710422
Record daily cardio and resistance training progress.

Count It Up Diet Journal
ISBN-13: 978-1500728410
Journal for recording calories and macronutrients on a daily basis plus sections for meal plans, and monthly progress.